LEND ME YOUR WINGS

LEND ME YOUR WINGS

POEMS BY
LILLO WAY

SHANTI ARTS PUBLISHING
BRUNSWICK, MAINE

Lend Me Your Wings

Published by Shanti Arts Publishing

Shanti Arts LLC
193 Hillside Road
Brunswick, Maine 04011
shantiarts.com

Interior and cover design by Shanti Arts Designs

Art by Rachel Brumer (Earthscape Series)
and used with her permission
www.rachelbrumer.com

Printed in the United States of America

ISBN: 978-1-951651-79-4 (softcover)
ISBN: 978-1-951651-80-0 (ebook)

Library of Congress Control Number: 2021936530

for
Bill McNeill

and for
Daniel and Alysandra

CONTENTS

ONE

FLYING

for my grandmother, Lillo Dillon of the Flying Dillons,
Barnum & Bailey Greatest Show on Earth, c. 1900

It's about your eyes, yours
   and your brother's, as you time
      your run up the rungs
         of the twin flimsy ladders.

It's about your fingers, catching
   and wrapping the trapeze bar,
      about the whoosh as he slings it
         from his platform perch.

It's about the platform
   and your soft-slippered feet
      as they push you from it
         into thick air.

It's about the air,
   warm there near the top
      of the big top, the smell
         of hot canvas, the taste

of your makeup melting.
   About the clips that must not fail
      to hold the chignon to your head,
         about the whalebone stays

of your corseted waist, the swell
   of your lungs above them,
      the cotton tights that want to bag
         at your knees, your knees over

your bar, your brother's over his,
  breathing measured to the music.
    It's about your arms stretched
      downward from the fly bar,

the sweep of your legs held tight together,
  the point of your feet, the certainty
    your hands *can* reach,
      will clasp wrists, your wrists

bruised with the seams
  of his fingers, then the letting go.
    It's about the letting go—his eyes,
      your arms, the trapeze, its song.

HIGH WINDS

Down in the abandoned duck blind, the mallards
heard the warning and battened themselves.

There is not so much as a crow in sight
and there's never not a crow in sight.

You could almost imagine the eagles had made
their way back to the endangered species list
and the herons had decided to go hungry.

But the gulls were born and bred to these swirling gusts
and as I stand watch on my fourth-floor balcony,
a group of seventeen swerve a curve off my right shoulder

and bank so low I have their backs and the dorsum
of their wings, and they are whiter than doves,
whiter than angels in their unison turning of thermals.

If Mark Morris choreographed birds, he'd have made
this phrase of movement and costumed it stark white
against a boiling dark backdrop just like this

and Busby Berkeley, infinite balconies above mine
would stand up, multiply himself by four dozen,
and give Mark a kaleidoscopic ovation

while I, no greater than a glass chip wedged
in a microscopic corner of the turning windscope,
would join in the deafening applause.

FROM THE WINGED VIRGIN OF QUITO, "THE DANCING MADONNA," TO BERNARDO DE LEGARDA, WOOD CARVER

venerated Ecuadorian sculpture (1734)

You made me sweat and weep and dance away
        my years on the surface of this earth. You
                put nothing between me and it but a snake—
        holiest of creatures because legless—who slithers
belly to belly with Mother Earth, skin-intimate.

I fling the blue shawl you gave me, swing
        my skirt, laugh faster, stomp higher, swerve
                and curve in a manner better suited to
a Hindu goddess than a Virgin Mary. But look now,

today you've carved feathers rippling
        from my scapula. Well, plume the serpent
                and wing my dancing feet! Feather my breast
and sprout a pair of pinions from my hips!

Give me wings that undulate heavier
        than a condor's, faster than a hummingbird's,
                more transparent than a cicada's, tinier
than a fairyfly's. And please, angle all these wings

in different and opposing directions, causing me to jig
        and hula, bellying my dance out of here, flying
                not straight up with the angels, but sideways
        with the dragonflies, swooping with the swallows,
flitting and staggering with the fritillaries.

MAPLE SEED POD I

with a wing like that
you could travel beyond
the biggest pond in this park

your tiny veins roadmap
routes out of here
with a wing like that

you could marry a moth
brush dusts and give birth
to a butterfly bush

if I nap long enough
in the grass under the maple
if I dream   if I snore

if I do nothing   you will
dance your dance   land
on my sleeping face

what makes a tree want to fly
leap from a bank run along
the beach waving its branches

you find a deep brown
of luscious earth damp
and hungry you settle

down until your lacy wing
is eaten and what's left waits
its lean dark eye unseen

I glue you to a scrap
of paper draw a horizon
you whisper sparrow

EQUESTRIENNE

There goes my Aunt Rosie walking down Market Street
     on her hands.

There's Aunt Rosie in a full split on the hot sidewalk,
     beaming for a neighbor's snapshot.

There she is dancing a solo in her living room,
     while singing "I'll Be Loving You Always"
     and "Sweetheart, Sweetheart, Sweetheart"
     in her lingering English accent.

My Aunt Rosie folds herself in half,
     her prat goes up in the air, she pastes her belly button
     to the front of those powerful thighs
     and each knee gets an eye
     when she reaches for a thick black skillet
     beneath the oven.

There's Rosie sewing my ballet costume
     as if it were all that mattered,
     tacking the point of the bodice in a *French tuck*
     rather than stitching it to the tulle.

     I do not forget while I am on stage that my costume
     is different from those of the other children.
     Mine has been sewn by the gorgeously coarse-faced
     Rosie who had danced on the bare back of a horse
     in a great three-ring circus in her day, a day
     she regretted leaving not for a moment, so far as I could tell.

There's Aunt Rosie singing a solo in front of our church congregation
     wearing a fitted knitted number,
     all muscle and fireplug strong and lifted up
     through the spine like a queen,

Who gladly presented me to the Dairy Queen—
     forbidden by my mother, her sister, the holy Alice,
     who condemned Rose for her ever-changing passions,
     while I silently begged the God of Alice
     how he might have made this error,
     giving me to her and not to my obvious mother,

Rosie, who in the circus museum wears soft golden boots
     in her arabesque on a trotting brown-and-white mare.

And now there's my Aunt Rosie
     under the field behind her empty bungalow,
     performing a series of perfect tinsicas
     for me and for the lady's slippers.

STARLETS

Eighteen starlings strung along a power cable.
Sunlings, really—day birds—shining blacker
than night in the light of the longest day,
all watching the same direction, as if danger
couldn't possibly approach from tailward.
A chorus line in a shallow proscenium theater,
each chorine staring straight downstage,
world's shortest-legged Rockettes,
shuffling a little up or down the line.
You figure it's the best they can do,
forgetting that their dance is all pent-up,
waiting, in the wings.

They leave the high-wire dance floor in a fugue.
A crowd of crows bursts into raucous cheers.

HOT TWELVE O'CLOCK

Biggest and baldest of eagles clutches a lunch
of seagull and screams ugly, muscles up
her black wings in a high V, as the mirrored
white chevron hang-glides from her talons.

Hot twelve o'clock allows itself to be fondled,
consoled, by a big cool gust, which has just
blown in through the doors and snatched
from the dining table what had been

a short stack of torn magazine pages—
poems too good to read once and let go—
and transformed it into a small flock
of gleaming dead gulls falling from thermals.

What bird, balcony, branch will catch the black
words on white paper: "Running Scared,"
"The Dog's Tooth," "Summer Grace,"
"What I Did With Your Ashes?"

MALHEUR

The owl of me swallowed you whole and swift.
   Only later the odd taste.
You carried small poison, but enough to serve.
   I unfurl my wings, hoot, screech.
Wind roughs my feathers' fading gold.
   The deep gut of me twists.
I know what the rat of you has done.
   Fur and bone pellets fall from my mouth.
The fatal liquor remains below.
   You did to me what others had done to you.
I gaze up from my nest.
   Raptors gather.

NOCTURNE WITH TALONS

One's a horse whinny, one a rooster crow,
   and one you'd swear
is the crazed warble of a loon. One
   a summer night's thousand insects,
another the scream of a banshee.
   They might be answering, however falsely,
the question, *Who?*
   But no one's asking.

If I've heard owls in the past,
   I didn't know enough to know them.
But in this hamlet, owls speak
   their speeches beyond the stage
of my three-feet-deep,
   three-centuries-old windowsill
and play all the parts,
   from tiniest chickadee
to giant snoring dragon.

Shakespeare claims such clamorous owls
   wonder at our quaint spirits,
mentions an owl that shrieks
   as we are born, an owl that cries
a warning when the ghosts stroll,
   and as the day's curtain falls,
an owl that bids us the very sternest
   good-night.

MAPLE SEED POD II

O double samara
O winged achene
your function: diaspora

dry fruit   drift fruit
shaped for spinning   born
in racemes corymbs umbels

your wing elongates
from your birdeye black satin
seed its filmy lid laced

and carried on the wind
twinned   you may yet
part company for flight

decreasing the odds
of getting lost   children
pry you   sport you on their noses

gyre gyre spring of life
papery crane   maple's origami
hundreds of thousands of you

so they say   from one tree
at one time   after this dream
of flying you sleep exhausted

sometimes for years
before waking up
in something else's body

Two

TRILOGY

1. Trifle

Once I wore a dress like a flower petal dropped on the naked
stamen of my dancer body. More than once I slipped the
narrow strap of it over my left shoulder and bending slightly,
fed my seated dinner guest his dessert. The guest then melted
like sorbet on a summer evening, and looked up at me as
if he'd seen god. Next, sure as spring follows winter, he fell
in love. It didn't matter who my guest was, and it certainly
didn't matter who I was, it happened this way every time,
after dinner, after wine.

2. Visiting My Aunt Reba, in Her Perfectly Content Apartment on the Chesapeake Bay Flats, for the First Time Since her Mastectomy

which she says wasn't nearly as bad as the shingles she'd had
two years before. She is not wearing the bra that holds her
prosthesis, but she tells me how amazingly much it weighs,
then goes to fetch it from her bedroom and places it, a beige
leaden wedge, in my hands so I may raise and lower it a few
times, in order to appreciate its gravity—I, of the teeny-
bopper tits that never, in subsequent years, bothered to rouse
themselves to aspirations of greater maturity, holding her
giant geometric substitute for a breast in my upturned palms,
looking into her familiar gray eyes, same color as her hair,
saying wow . . . wow . . . and imagining what it would be like
to strap that object onto my chest every day and sally forth
into the great weird world.

3. I Know Not Seams

My shirts have turned seamy side out, baring their stitches.
The fresh ones in my flesh tolerate only the type of seamless
smooth found in the newborn section of department stores.
Nipples made electric at the dimple-end of a tight-lipped grin
that radiates across the breast and rips lightning under the
arm. I'm scored and skivered, touch me not, not even you,
slightest breeze.

EMPTY DRESS

Oh sure I've passed knickers on my daily walks
        here a condom there a sock
but today as I enter what would be
        a clearing were it not garbled in vinca vines
an entire empty dress is spread out
        on the thousands of shiny leaves
a flowered dress as if it had bloomed
        right there from seed
and my eyes refuse not to see a naked woman
        smoothed on top of the many-colored silk
staring at a black-bearded fully-clothed man
        until he turns and she climbs on his back
slipping herself between his shirt and tailcoat
        locking her toes in his cummerbund
and as he lopes away into the woods
        she reaches for his huge top hat
slides it down over her small head
        until the brim rests on her collarbones
having entirely forgotten she came in wearing a dress.

CHARMING A SNAKE IN THE WOODS

She points to it with the big toe of her left foot—
  a small green stocking garter.
The life-force fired from her metatarsal
  stops it dead in its curvaceous dust canal.

She plants her right foot perpendicular
  to the snake's ruler-length, invites it to pass
under the impossibly high arch, the golden gate
  of her golden-brown foot.

And it does. It flows like water under her sole,
  the molecules it has disturbed touch her skin
like breath from an infant.

As it emerges, sunlight grabs its bracelet surface,
  emerald as jewels on a dragon's back.
She reaches down and it glides onto the promised land
  of her hand, it hisses *yes yes* to this strange plane.

She brings it toward her mouth as if to kiss it
  and there are whispers in the woods—the switch
of a ground squirrel's tail, the flit of a sparrow
  near her copper-birch arms.

She strokes the snake smooth along her cheek,
  raises her hand to her head, gently settles it in her hair
and she is a minor Medusa—one punk-green strand
  slithers down the knolls of her vertebrae
and over her precise buttock, pausing a millisecond
  in the valley at the back of her knee.

It knows where earth is, where's home. It flashes
  her calf, circles once about her ankle, and disappears—
born and bred to be lost among leaves, grasses,
  and anything green.

THE FLASH

Look here, a mere inch stripe
of fire orange sunset holding its own
under a bumpy blue curtain
socked between the great-dome sky
and the puny line of Seattle buildings
beyond the window-sill.

Just when I am content with this slender
golden Cleopatra snake of color,
my eyes are struck with a stabbing's-worth
of candlepower as the sun slides herself
right into that skinny strip.

I'm telling you that disc's shining a path
across the lake from there to me
worthy of any buxom harvest moon.
But here's the kicker: At the end of her short show,
she winks an unmistakable *rayon vert*—
magical reward for willing one's eyes
not to blink during her last second of visible life.

And then—I know you won't believe this—
the green lingers, snuggles girlishly
against an upended skyline rectangle,
and tosses out a pinch of lime juice
to the lake's ripple tips.

You are going to tell me green flashes
happen only over oceans and so I thought.
Never in all my years of watching the sun
disappear behind Jersey City did I see
anything even slightly verdigris,

and certainly not the sexy shade of green
she sometimes likes to flash
just at her final exit, ensuring we won't forget,
that we'll watch every single night,
hoping she'll show it again.

GLOAMISH

The big red door is licked back so the flies come
and go as they please. The peach of a sun
has unplucked itself onto the backside of a tree
and dangles by a bungee cord stem. Twilight

gushes in, a cross between gooey and billowy,
heads less than straight up the stairs, expands
into the bedroom, spreads itself over the furniture,
then turns to me.

It curls along my limbs and face, showing the courtesy
to leave a little breathing space around my nostrils. I rest
against its bulbous volume. Together we allow the evening
to serenade us—a jumbo jet

booming a little something from *Götterdämmerung*
as it dives its charges home before dark, the brutal upswing
of a floored car, a bus's asthmatic wheeze, the barking
of summer children—woven together by an obbligato

of finches and sparrows, robins and jays. How do the birds
keep it up in the ears of all this noise? My guess is
they've mustered their competitive spirits and cranked up
the volume—double forté and twice the number

of instruments. Twilight is overstaying its welcome here
in my north country city. It and I grow weary of one another.
Finally we give up and settle down on the floor together.
In the soft, dank carpet, we caress, make a little love.

GREAT BLUE

Why have you, crotchety old man,
        stalked me, lithe young woman,
stretched your heron's neck over me
        and watched—unmoving,
unmoved in your absolute possession?

You, still as a woodcut until
        your shaggy-sparse overcomb
fluffs loose in the swampwind,
        you'll wait forever
if forever it takes.

You, for whom flying is to unfold, painstakingly,
        ancient wings hardly yours—
your ancestors' wings torn, worn
        rags, gray and dirty blue, uncranked.
My breath comes short as I glimpse you drop them,
        impossibly heavy, then barely
haul them up again.

You, who exaggerate those skinny legs
        to walk the shore as twigs
would walk were they able,
        until underbelly deep, you meditate
before your lightning strike.

Why have you staked your weirdness
        into my neck knees heart, my hollow bones,
my salt grass hair?

FRAME THE MOON

Furred out, cased, paned and trimmed,
the opening of a window.

From my position here on the floor
in supine half-spinal twist,

my quarter-revolving eye catches
a perfectly sliced-in-half moon centered

in the upper right corner of the upper
left pane of a window blued by a sky

somewhere between baby-boy daytime
and electric-transvestite midnight—

the perfect globe cleavered by
a celestial butcher-boy—

the first half of hope, not the last,
depending, I suppose, on your viewing point,

mine being spine suppliant to floor,
floor kissing earth and holding the kiss,

earth sucking me hard, the half-moon
mullioned and muntined,

one four-millionth of a light-year away,
beaming me up and off from here—

half an inkling that, when the bones wave
their white phalanges of surrender

to whatever pulls us down—some unthing,
some weightless, scentless, tasteless,

wan thing, draws me up into a moon's
glowy, showy, half-assed bliss.

BROKEN

1.

At night, I lie still as glass, as if a bell jar
casket arched over me—glass over glass.

Light shoots through the window glass,
then through the net that keeps the flies off,
if there were flies, and I startle awake, splintering
what I thought was far more than a dream,
but within seconds isn't even that, is nothing,
less than glass, less than light or lightness,
its vision blown thin.

2.

Through the closed window, fish leaves silver
on a willow tree. Through the open one,

I hear birds, clear as glass, in sounds we call song
or we call language, and which the birds call
nothing. One flies into the bedroom. Is it alarmed
to see me wasted, but steaming the glass, swimming
through dreams that sliver and melt like ice,
then evaporate? Tomorrow, when it comes again,
the bird will break its neck on transparency.

3.

I'm awake now. A mirror prisms light
in whole notes across the wallpaper.

When I reach for my glasses, I brush the invisible
water glass from the table and it bursts
into shards. Some glitter, beckoning my feet,

others hide for days or weeks, then slip into my toes,
mix with my blood, turn themselves to rubies,
while the soprano who lives in my radio
shatters a high C.

ANGEL HILL CEMETERY

Purple bells touch the names
of people I sprang from but never
knew. Hyacinth against stone
markers, fragrance strong enough
to make a five-year-old swoon.

I wonder if the buried can feel
Aunt Reba's swollen knees
pressing against their chests
as she works the trowel?
Watching her muscled love,

I imagine they can see
the dimming sun, taste
the light rain, smell the intense
death of these grave flowers
brown by next Sunday.

When Easter falls in March, the earth
is stubborn-hard under her fingers.
But when it arrives overdue
in late April, it yields soft—reeking
of life and afterlife in one breath.

Reba bows before their names—
mother, father, uncle, brother.
Some church-god may have escorted
them here, but if there's any god today,
it's Aunt Reba, broke-kneed, benevolent.

She carried the plants delicately
up Angel Hill Road, cradling them
in her arms. But on the way back down,
she lets me hold the empty brick pots,
her gardening gloves folded damp inside.

She watches as my fingers slide
along the brown curds clinging
to the terracotta. She watches
as I hold the dirt to my nostrils,
then place it on my tongue.
She says nothing as I swallow,
nothing as I swipe
four dun fingers across the chest
of my lavender Easter dress.

MANDOLIN SEA

Sandals line up outside a temple
        or outside a dance studio where your ears
                fill with bells or the banging
        of an out-of-tune upright that drowns

out the rain whose colors are too pale
      to notice, whose drops fly on the breeze,
        and when they reach a river rich
            with the sweat of martyrs and jesters,
     they swim, as if blessed by heroes' crosses
          or fools' cross-garters.

When you hear a glass harmonica,
    prism in the high notes, fish-eyes
       in the low, no matter if you cheated at math
            or lied to a lover or staggered
        through your days, a mandolin
        will find you, and though you hold it

       backwards, your right hand around its neck,
a dirge of incense and a jingle of lollipops
        accompanies your body as you dive below
          the busy rain of the music's surface,

breathing like a fish now, singing like the sea.

Barn Lit by a Duck Egg

1.

O spheroid O perfect thing
O white (in this case) O brown (in another)
O thin shell transparent prehistoria
transporting splendent from one place to another
from inside to outside where we crouch
on these rotting wet boards in the pig-reeking dark

from nest to table rolling light through veins
through skin thin as paper tissue
you issue morning day fire I've named you
Edison little Eddie Egg I don't know
what's going on inside there
and I'm not about to crack
the only albuminous source in this lumenless room
smelling of goat and fowl

2.

egg glowing still warm
from the heart-beating body
of your mother heating my palm
while frosting it in duck dung egg
of lopsided midnight bottom first
you present and will balance
if conditions are right O candling egg

if only I could be as perfect as you
one organic smooth-skinned
beauty with no sticking out appendages
no awk-angled fingers and toes no nose
I'll roll your luminosity in my palms switch
from right to left toss you like a juggler
and catch you in my lamp-lit mouth

3.

there's nothing an egg can't be
it births a thousand mythologies
it pours out the breaking point
smells like the pouring paste
camouflaging the sulfur until
the heat's on and stays on

little milky knot of attachment
tomorrow I'll go ahead and eat you
or strain you out
then whisk away the sun and its gilt
dilute it with white reason
gobble you down

4.

a child finds a cracked egg
saves it in a shoe box
and swoons her first real swoon
when she rediscovers it weeks later
at the top of the closet behind
Mister Potato Head medusafied
O egg's swan song I slip

rock's auk's egg between my legs
and guide it in no strings attached
and I'm a lit body a Keith Haring lamp
radiating Burchfield vibrations
in creams and sunflower listen
music of the night from an egg
Messiaen could see it
and we can too if we lean close

rest the egg in the pinna of our ear
it will sing us until we wake up
we'll dance to it and sway our Daffy Duck tails
among the horsetail and lamb's tongue
hold hands with Burchfield's ears
and Messiaen's eyes link arms
with all the synergists living in secret places
where nothing brings on everything
and everything happens at once

5.

it's raining on this duck egg now
but not enough to put out its light
just polish it up slip wheels
under it and roll it down the line
like a new Volkswagen Bug still
sticky inside from its not-birth

backlit road map of the pointed world
there you see it the light
tracing an unpredictable path
then bursting through
irradiating the barn

THREE

CHILD ON THE DELTA SHORE

she's never here without the dog,
only excuse for escape *walk the dog*.
out the door she marvels that such
a home as hers would have a dog.

she thanks the dog, spelling it backwards
and frontwards. she thinks stifling house,
she means *house on fire*. dog digs up
the wrung wings of a water bird,

tangled in shad tails. beneath them,
a beaked skull, giftwrapped in seaweed
and the snake roots of last year's water
lilies. the child's thumbs smooth the bones

and though she's never seen a bird skeleton
before, she knows the gull shape of it
the girl shape of it, knows
I am this bird.

her chin floats up. her scapulae lift,
elbows, wrists, fingertips fly
far from her sternum, reach beyond
the cold, catch a thermal.

a gray gull's wingtips are lit silver
in solos of light—salty hunger
of its scream reed-pitched for fish flesh.
not an ugly screech to her ears.

where gulls are, open sea isn't far.
she imagines a paint-peeled boat,
dog perched in its bow, the alphabet
spilled across its stern, *out of here*.

About a Delta

What is it about a delta that never leaves us alone,
   we who were born in one of the bulrushed triangles,
      speaking a variant of the English tongue,
   no knowledge of Greek, the land's shape traced
beneath the arches of our feet, unrecognized?

What is it about a river snake, backed blue-green,
   bellied in brown, swallowed by a bay or gulped
      by a gulf, circling itself into a low, humid caldron,
         finger-stirred or stilled before yielding, manly
      or womanly, to the great oceansea, which some of us
would never see? What about marsh and mudflats,
               fishstink and waterlilies?

Our bellies full on the shad side or the crayfish,
   we were lean, every one of us, nourished
      by creatures from basin and bay, and what we grew
   in our backyards and what grew there on its own—
herbs we called weeds, and spring onions.

Low-tide river flats the first air of our first inhale,
   and should we travel continent after continent,
      we will recognize it in the marsh shallows
         of every delta in every county or country
      that has one. Fishbones, shells and shorebirds,
cattails and longrasses, the similar cries of geese
               and of humans.

SLEEPWALKER

you walk home
        like a dog traveling night
        after night back across states
    you return to where it began
you never see me your fingerprints
        oil no walls your knees
        slip by chairs no curtains
            brush your flannels you steer clear
            we might be ballroom dancers
        for a moment your palm rests in my left
    gently I place my right on your waist
        when moonlight crosses the bridge
            of your nose you begin to hum the way
                humming might sound from inside the womb
                    your kitchen toes touch only the white
                        tiles never the black
                    you sleepstack
                the kettle
            the pot
        stop short
    of fire

1955 RAUSCHENBERG BED

Pull on a thread and the bed
unmakes itself.

Tug a stitch and initiate
an unquilting bee.

Last night your hair fell out
and scribbled all over the pillow,

mouse-gray head hairs
dangling white sheet threads,

each hair crossing out
fibers by fives.

You've left your stingray
mouth here too,

its bottom lip sticked
snapper red.

Down the covers slide mucus
blood and moonrays in a bedhead afterbirth,

past sheep white as sheets
against sky,

wagging their shirttails
behind them.

You've made your bed now
(hang it all) on the wall.

What a life we've slept here—hair
blood and sun in the sheep-blinking earth,

thick and glorious
in your wet-paint dreams.

MATISSE MODEL

you and I Henri we like keeping the door
in sight   I'm drawn to what you draw
the door   the window

you look down on the Bay of Nice
without going down   the fish are gold
and in a jar   good to know the unwieldy world
is out there   good to tuck it in a box

personally I like keeping one hand
on the doorknob   one eye on you
behind the apples and asphodels
behind the silence   an empty violin case

you know you could leave
the deep the rich the warm
configured textures saturated
with the perfume of paints

if you wanted to   but you don't
so I'll go gladly and report back
tell you everything   slipping
from my robes   stretching out

on the tapestries   while in the corner
your wife's face flattens in sleep
along a table   you smell the salt
wind coming off me

your brush strokes slow
voluptuize me fur-first sliding
from my armchair toward you

BACKBEND

Looking upside down cumulo
cirrus clouds white on sky blue
linoleum in a backbend drinking water
as I saw a girl do on the talent hour
and knew I could too.

Mother wincing twisting
a nervous wedding ring recalls
the circus family she escaped
wide-eyes me whom she has strained
to train in domestic arts. From here I see

the undersides of things kitchen
table turquoise where legs bend to be screwed in
salmon upholstery pulled and tacked beneath chairs
cabinet bottoms where feathery paint strokes quit early
avocado-green blender rising like a skyscraper.

Ceiling's a floor as white as a circus tent
carte blanche to all that transpires below and above.
I've drunk the water in the paper cup tilted with my teeth.
I rock back and forth to spring upright—sky and clouds
once again below me where they belong.

HEY HO NOBODY HOME

frozen grass flats as far as your eye will see
under an old weeping willow stripped tearless
the sky an aluminum sheet prone on top of it

foursquare house where the mother is doing
whatever she does after announcing in no uncertain terms
it's time for the children to get fresh air

if you enter the brick house kitchen
and prop up the stove's surface by its pin-arm
you'll find a tiny pilot light bluish sliding toward an orange end

that's the size of the life in my otherwise empty snowsuit
propped in front of four nailed planks damming wet sand
flecked with desiccated scraps torn from pale leaves

watching the brother who by unfathomable means
knows what to do with a sandbox carve roads with edge of shovel
drive metal cars while roaring puttering brake-screeching
he not as straight-jacketed as I

cotton-batted Melton wool appendages unjointed
suspender escapes shoulder leggings slip to knees
throat-gripping cap strap bulges with each swallow

fingers and toes as ivory-numb as the keys of the spinet
you'll find against the staircase in the living room
of the stifling warm house where my sheep-smelling wrappings
will be peeled away at last

and the pilot light who is me will slip
vaporously up the stairs and into the dolls
on the shelf in the blue bedroom

PEARLS BEFORE SWINE

If it happened to be summer,
   she went around slamming windows
to keep the neighbors from hearing
   her berate, at the full capacity
of her well-trained voice, her young
   toothpick-limbed children, my brother
and me, who gave excellent impressions
   of people suffering from starvation,

but who, in reality, had simply burned
   our calories in adrenaline rushes
and nervous fidgets, biting the lining
   of our cheeks and twisting clumps
of our hair—or my brother's specialty—
   a tic of the neck and chin, as if
wearing a necktie noosed too tightly.

Once the window sashes stopped
   reverberating, she lit into
her "ungrateful wretches" for whom
   she "worked her fingers to the bone,"
casting her "pearls before swine."

And what thanks did she get?
   Not so much as a "well done
my good and faithful servant."
   If we thought childhood was meant to be
"one grand and glorious good time,"
   we had another thought coming.

When the storm of her high holy furor
   had passed, she rushed forward,
her spirits pirouetting on a dime,
   to embrace us in her ample body,
declaring us "Mama's darling angels,"
   "best children who ever trod the earth."
And so it was, amid one woman's flair
   for alliteration and biblical paraphrasing,
we received our sentimental education.

INFIRMARY

The childhood of this morning's memory is filled with bees.
    Bees air-kissing the arbutus, bees rolled tight inside rose petals,
bees on plants named for butterflies, bees bouncing around blades
    of grass, striping yellow and black across their green.

When the lawnmowers choked, when the boat motors cut out,
    when the cicadas quit rattling, the chant of a hundred saffron-robed
bees droned through the heat waves and into the star-shaped shadows
    of the sugar gum trees. These bees were all sound and sting.

Except, that is, for the maimed ones.

How carefully I cultivated a precise technique by which I pressed
    the sole of my shoe, just so, against the furry body of each bee,
injuring the creature without killing it, that it might be sent,
    in a screaming matchbox ambulance, to the emergency room

of Insect Memorial Hospital, where I, as attending doctor,
    would nurse it, and those who had suffered similar accidents,
back to health with the caring and indulgent attention that only
    the pure of heart can deliver to patients in their time of need.

And while morbidity and mortality were, of course, inevitable,
    many in my charge recovered fully enough to fly away
from the rehabilitation pavilion of my front yard and resume
    their lives as highly functioning members of the universal hum.

CICADA CANTICLE

Listen,
they chant three songs
      in hollow-belly voices
loud enough to damage human ears,
      while flick-wing clicks
syncopate the flexing
      of their gut-wall drums,
singing out their secrets
      hidden underground
for seventeen years.

      We kids hear the ancestors
calling. We smack together
      any two twigs, strike a tree trunk,
shake leaves strong as a storm,
      whisk a switch through thin air,
rain sound down, catch it
      in a shell pod gourd rattle,
sizzle-without-words.

      We join the dance
that overnight leaves the earth
      silent layered in translucent shells.
Our bare foot-soles improvise
      a new music, tuneless.
We crush the husks to dust
      against a cracked pavement
in our small hard yards.

NOSTALGIA FOR DAPPLED SHADE

you smell moisture sucking up the sizzle of wet tar
        I poke my big toe in the road's
hot bubble and wear the plastic
        black cap for the next three days

where the point-tip leaves make only circles in the grass
        you spread the army blanket khaki
under the sugar maples so blades spring up
        through the dark rim of its cigarette burn

I catch the twirling seed propeller before it lands
        in the blonde vinyl of a doll's wig coming unglued
(ants walk delicately across our shins
        toward the smell of sweating sweet tea)

you squeeze the Chinese yew berries and roll
        their tiny pits between your fingers
make paste of the scarlet slime
        and use it to fasten the colors of a paper chain

I ride my ears like rafts on the rising surface
        of locust clatter then sink them heavy
into the silent pause between
        verses of their rattlestick song

you press your itchy face against the damp
        wool felt of the animal who lived to be its source
in the good old summertime and recline
        under the sky-holes that bleach our lashes bald

                sun's down   wind's died
                        breeze won't make it
                        through the screens
                                of the sleeping-porch   tonight

FOUR

OFF BALANCE

I was that kid

who stumbled over mourning doves hidden
                    beneath unpruned Chinese yews
          over pet rat Charles   over the damp summer
                    hump in the carpet

who stumbled through scales in third-grade chorus
                    was asked to mouth the words
     and never told my proud parents as I stumbled after them
                    my shoes eating my socks heel-first.

I was the one

who stumbled over my lines after Kenny forgot his
                    and one by one the whole cast followed suit
          until we realized we'd just skipped the entire second act

who was wise enough at my wedding not to risk
                    walking down an aisle
          but not wise enough to choose a fitting groom

who stumbled at the cemetery my hands full of earth
                    and was grateful beyond expression
                    not to have fallen in with my mother.

Then I stumbled

into you one Christmas Eve   knocked the cup of sorrows
                    out of your hand
          and threw your arms around me for the rest
                    of my bumbling life.

COME LIVE WITH ME

You won't find a wall and ceiling perpendicular.
Every board, crown-molding and seam,
once right-angled, has gone to wonk.

Counters, where I'll invite you to rest your shopping bags,
are a half-bubble off plumb. Watch the lemons roll.

The rose-colored roses have dried and faded to tan,
but the paintings hold their jungled tangle of colors,
bright ones.

The faucets won't stop weeping, rust
has made a thousand pinholes in the pipes,
and the furnace has taken up singing.

Window frames have loosened their grip on the panes—
a cracked one fractures the weedy garden—you may feel
a draft at your neck.

I've emptied the ashes and swept the hearth for you,
but chimney swifts have made a home in their name-place.

The upholstery's gone too saggy or too hard
and the floor is cold. We'll lie on the bed.
Turn one another to spoons.

PERFECT PITCH

The ancient yogis chanted "om" in order to bring themselves
into harmony with the universe. —harmonymanual.com

I hum good morning to the first electric bus at 5:45, the first
jet plane at 6. I hum the thud of the *New York Times*
on the porch deck, and the roar of its deliverer's getaway car.

In the kitchen, I hum the white pitch of the furnace,
the wolf pitch of the microwave, the steep pitch
of the refrigerator door left ajar.

In the front yard, I hum the whine of my neighbor's
leaf blower, the backing-up beep of a garbage truck.
I hum alarm, pitch perfect.

I hum for all I'm worth to gentle my struggle in accepting
the way things are. I hum to drown out my most excellent
judgments, my spot-on critiques.

It's December now, so I'm humming the tired carols. I adjust
up to sharp and down to flat. I hum lullabies to machines,
hymns to *deus ex machina*.

Lying in bed, I hum a Mozart quartet to the neighbors'
late partying. And in the long middle hours of the night,
when you are snoring, I hum every love song I know.

SKY DANCE

We drove to the moon and then under it.

Turned out to be a belly dancer. First
the belly itself, severally buttoned, then
her face half-veiled, then a golden finger-cymbal,
twing twing, we both heard it ring
into thin night air.

We spread the army blanket on the roof
of the car, tried ways of braiding four legs
while keeping our moon-blanched faces
pointing straight up at the sky's floorshow.

We droned, we drummed, we buzzed our lips,
whining a high-pitched arabesque as she slid
the veil lower, then gradually slipped
her diaphanous skirts into piles
on the black dance floor.

We gazed at her nakedness until we were blinded,
we let our eyelids drop and in the silence,
we covered ourselves in her castoff costume,
gone cool and wet and gray.

SCHLAF, LIEBLING, SCHLAF

A snuffle. Just the minorest kerfluffle
   between your mouth and nose.

Next a snorfle. A baby bunny of a snore.
   Then a snort, hardly a knuffle,

leading to a wee Swedish snarka,
   followed by *eine kleine schnarchenmusik.*

Now silence, complete and sweet.
   My lungs exhale fully, I will sleep.

But the silence elongates,
   and you no longer are breathing.

I turn my head and watch unblinking.
   Nothing. I'm rehearsing my call to 911,

when comes a strangled mew
   of pain and warning, before what seems

to be a score composed for a horror movie
   erupts from your resonating chambers.

Quadruple forté, basso profundo,
   it soars, bouncing from ceiling to floor.

I leap up and make for the hall
   while you go to work. You build

a wall of sound around the bedroom,
   snore by ever more complex snore.

A Sleeping Beauty of a wall, but no
    mere tangle of bramble and thorn,
        penetrable by any insomniac prince.

Yours, pure granite schnauben—tall,
    dense, and seemingly radioactive.

I approach the doorway but am repelled
    by a clotted force-field of guttural static—

a vibrating steamroller of noise,
    more machine than animal.

A bulldozer of sound. A demolition derby,
    crushing the very concept of slumber.

I head for the hinterland
    of the office/guest room, press a braid rug

along the bottom of the door—a bulwark
    against your aspirated bullhorn—

and pull the quilt over my head.
    I adore you. I unsnore you.

THE LOONIES

Those Celtic monks who copied
at narrow tables on rocky islands
in bad weather, wearing itchy brown robes
whitened with gannet poop? I'm them.

The 1940s recording stenographer—
knees together, pencil skirt,
chunky heels, tortoise shell glasses,
only woman in the room,
click-clacking away? I'm her.

I don't think anything up.
I just sit and copy what the loonies
from on high are whispering in my ear.
I lose my sleep to them,
find their minds abnormal.

The loonies may come as dreams
or wake me from their dreams,
pummeling me about the temples
with their leather boxing gloves,
while I do their transcribing
in the dot-green lights of the coffeepot-
computer-stove-stereo-telephone-
microwave-mercuryvapormoon.

They speak whacko clear through the wax
of my earplugs, they dance
my twitching muscles, polish my pate
and blow Gabriel's horn
right through my nose. They ache
my back sitting up in bed.

One thing I'll say for the loonies,
they've got rhythm and I notate it
in quarters, sixteenths, accelerandos,
ritards, and hemi-demi-semi-quavers.

They tap on my soles,
cant songs in my clavicles,
transport me into the dawn.

AT LEAST FOR TONIGHT

you'll deep those atoms. they'll swirl and settle.
drops on the bloom side of a parasol, a parapluie,
a beside-sun, beside-rain, not against.

in bed I'll cup my hand around your roundness,
cells plumped with fat but not, in this day's tidings,
with cancer, not this year.

when I sprawl over you, as you nap on your back,
you are my extrafirm beautyrest. I am not your blanket.
I'm a bobcat scrambling our connective tissue.

you say I'm not hurting you, but I know you'll put up
with pain to be this close to another animal.
skin pretending to be our only barrier.

we're going to lie down, one day, the way
we did today, when we're too tired to go on.
weight of your big head. my neck and cheek

your pillow. as you surrender, the container
that holds your thoughts drops a millimeter farther
into my jugular and jaw.

fear, our dominant emotion, gone. control,
our dominant action, over. what if we'd let go
earlier, spent decades lying here, in this place

which looks a lot like how we'd imagined it.
in your sleep, you smile the perfect smile.
one I've never seen before.

FLOATERS

Eye floaters are caused by age-related changes as the vitreous becomes more liquid. —healthteam.com

Six bats like broken umbrellas zigzag up your right eyeball
    leave behind three haystacks
        that repeat the way your forehead creases
    when you raise one eyebrow to look
        at the lavalamp of a dozen amoebas
    bouncing gently off your retina
        into the ivory holes that have been cut
    in a length of black silk the shape
        of the demi-cups of your brassiere
    which lounges on our bedspread
        where whale sperm squiggle
    over a fine scrim of what
        might be called no-see-ums
    except that you do
        above all of which an ebony crow sheers
    across your dirt-specked window
        balances on the southwest corner
and twitches its tail against the convergence
        of your crow's feet.

Here between Day and Night

A plump robin turns its seed eye
   on me suspicious, then agrees I'm not
      worth betting on.

The path lights, strangled by a plant
   called archangel, click on
      and the seeper hoses begin to weep.

A white-crowned sparrow's melody repeats
   and is rejoined with all the notes transposed,
      syllables articulated in the western flare.

A neighbor's hands touch piano keys
   as if she were their lover—her favorite
      song without words.

I stand up in the backache garden
   and share in the summer evening's relief
      at being granted the gift of long shadow.

NIGHT RITES

Check the locked doors, fill
   the glass with filtered water,
open the window a crack
   to the rigid night air.
Wash my body clean,
   lotion its lined face, ointment
its dry eyes. Inhale slowly
   and hold the breath, exhale
more slowly, repeat. Set out
   the earplugs and eye mask,
count the blessings:
   son, daughter, you,
two teachers, many friends.
   Count them backwards,
then count the loved dead.
   Pray for dreamless sleep
which never comes
   so pray for quotidian dreams—
no black stallions
   nor their night mares—
a night with no terror, no regrets.
   The house will not burn,
the phone will not ring
   with dead-of-night news.
Stack the pillows against the odds.

MARQUEZ NIGHT

Stained tea towel, charcoal bleeding into mustard,
    an umber edge holding the grime design together,
hung askew over the oven door handle
    in a garbage-rank closet of a flat
in the poorest street of an old town—that's what is
    the yellowish thing that calls itself a summer sky
hanging a few meters above my head
    and low pressuring me to fall into love
in the time of cholera where I become
    the sinking stinking still air, where I am
the last bird not to die in the fetid drying river,
    where I hear my ghost-voice calling
like a manatee mother to her missing children
    late in the last night of a landscape scraped empty
of trees and their shadows, moonlight staining the river
    yellow, the banks yellow, the only boat yellow,
the moon itself the final exit—small round aperture—
    through which I will, watch me now, escape.

ELEGY: A DANCE

You ask to walk the cedar-green path
      behind your house   to feel the needles
            of cool air pricking your cheeks
                  one more time

I trail you watching and ready
      you fall backwards as if melting
            your forearms sink against mine
                  until we are elbow-in-elbow

I step into you and slip my feet under yours
      soles curve over arches   toes over toes
            in this manner we turn and pick our way
                  two left feet   two right

Your body arches   pitches away from me
      I catch it as it crests
            steady you into your bird steps
                  and when they wobble   net you in again

Only now you've begun the dropping
      you slump I grab   hip ribs
            you sink I lift   clavicle shoulder
                  you collapse I clasp   neck temple

Down we slide together you come to rest
      in my thighs   improbably laughing
            sun is pressing our shadows
                  flat and broad as you go still

A wing slides across your lids
      your eye-light narrows
            smaller   black
                smaller   out

FIVE

APPROPRIATION

If I were an artist I'd paint this room,
a living room it is and one in front of which
I am entitled to put the first-person singular possessive,

as if I were the lighting designer who created
this morning sunshine and divided it
by fifty-six mullioned panes, the dyer
who spilled it across the fabric of the furniture,
the refinisher who varnished it on oak floors
which someone, a lifetime ago, troubled to inlay
with a double dark border,

as if I were one of a dozen children
who sat to countless dinners at what is now
a library table, into which I did not grind
my first food stains, nor apply the paint
still flecking its underside spring green.

Oh I've read the bright books lining the end wall
but didn't write one of them, nor did I design
their jackets or make their paper from trees,
mix the ink, set the type.

And I did not weave the rich complex rug
in rich complex Afghanistan,
or wear the Sarawak basket on my back
in the forests of Borneo, nor was I the animal
who gave its skin for the lid.

It wasn't I who freed the African stool from a trunk
with rough tools to bend its knees bowlegged
between brown earth and brown sky,

but it is the flesh of my back
this morning sun's a radiant heater to,
and if the sun grows too hot it's my sweat,
and it's my broken face slivered
in the eighteenth-century mirror,
fire-singed and thinned.

JOSEPHINE OF THE FIELDS

Come on out, Josephine, come out
of your log cottage at the edge of the long-needled pines
that drape the roof, turning the shingles green,
the trees themselves tinted blue in the light
of the *Ed Sullivan Show*.

You, watching the mahogany console,
put down your long-necked Schlitz,
rise from your patchouli-warmed, cigarette-cozied spot
under the dark cracked beams, and take me

up the narrow stairs to a bed nook where you
have sprinkled violet toilet water on pillow feathers
so I might sleep to the sound of semitrailers
straining gears on the hillroad. I'm asking you,

Josephine of hollyhocks and marigolds,
set down the fishing pole and give me
the strong brown hand that in the morning
trembled nervous to braid a young girl's hair.

Come, Josephine, stretch yourself on the davenport
exhausted, and read me chapters in *Old Yeller*
while the spaniel named for Tom Sawyer
naps on the braided oval rug. Come here,

dress me as a bride in your window curtains
and pose me in the chestnut-secreting sedge
where I, solemn, grip my marigold bouquet
as you kneel behind your Brownie camera.

And quick now climb down the tractor
to clomp your boots through rufous fields,
your wooded creeks and cowlicks,
before they are transformed

> into rows of small, identical, white houses—
> almost at the very second your lids
> last lower over those blind
> green Josephine eyes.

MARYLAND WATERMAN

Wood-frame screen door waffles in the breeze
of memory, the rusted hook of its eye dangling,
no longer quite able to reach its destination:
keep us all safe in this fisherman's bungalow
built at street level, now somewhat below.

On the edge of the shad-fragranced kitchen,
the screen opens a bit, loosely closes, opens wider,
bangs shut, causing people-headed milk bottles
to rattle in their 4-pack on the brick stoop
that overlooks boat hulls turned upside-down
on sawhorses, between hills of canvasback decoys.

By the time the old cherry tree spatters its patchy shade grass,
the wild roses have gone to hips
and the rot of grapes dizzies the songbirds,
duck-blinds—reed-new and cattail-fresh—will be back in water
and my grandfather's blue eyes, bleached nearly white,
will squint at the sky, foretell the weather.

No waste—not fuel, not food, not words.
Simple this followed by simple that,
church on Sunday without knowing why,
and a brief sit in the tight parlor in a house with no living room,
living not being something to accomplish inside four walls,
not when there are fish and ducks, a river and a bay,
mud, and thick rubber boots up to this waterman's shoulders.

THE TILEMAKERS

Provence 2018

they've been centuries at it
molding fitting roof tiles
random-not-random patterns
passed from père to fils
to père to fils to perfection

the earliest ones   so it is said
were formed on a person's thigh
hence the rounding hence
the taper at one end

thigh tiles the palest ones
rounded over the creamy thigh
of the tilemaker's young wife
the burnt orange ones laid hard
on the young man's own August thigh

the ashen ones on the thighs of Grandpère
as he surrenders to the woolen blanket
spread on the floor of his wooden cradle-bed
his thigh and the rest of him soon to go to ashes

even while his grey freckled tiles continue
to press against the blanched innocent
the sun-burning youth earth
and body and color this evening

slicked to a high varnish by a hard
but graceful rain darkened riched-up
only to be drained to a bleach
by tomorrow morning's sun

CAMPANA

Diamond contact of mallet to metal,
a single church bell breaks the dark morning
into bronze bits, the greening evening
into one hundred lemon pieces,
and the house is lit bright
by sound.

Strikes diminish to nudges so gentle
the breeze snatches them
from the oval windows of my ears
before they can slide down
the helix banisters waiting inside.
I pretend to hear the fading quavers, follow
them out the door into the quicksilver valley,
until I'm counting only my heartbeats
in the bottomland.

I imagine the striking one, trudging
up spiral stairs or leaping them
three at a time, reaching
for the wooden mallet, releasing
the one-note song of a one-legged girl
in a flared skirt embellished with scallop shells,
who vanquishes tempests, cleans the unclean,
and with the clang of her heavy metal,
dispels demons.

All vapor and mineral under the corbels,
blind chime of a 15th-century bell,
from campanile to loggia to grotto to girls
in the gladiola fields, to ants
in the underbellies of bluebells,

to bees in the umbels of onion and dill,
then traveling underground to knell,
half-muffled, a soul's
journey home.

Hung dead they call it, fixed
to a headstock without lever, wheel,
or rope for swinging. Hung dead
until reincarnated by a hammer held
in the hollow of a callused hand,
it wakes, singing its bell-metal prayer
from shoulder to waist, through lip
and out a surprised round mouth—
now   now   now   this ring   this one

THE OCEAN IS RAINING IN PORTICELLO

It's raining knives and forks frogs and ropes
halyards halberds cords and threads
in Porticello Sicily
and the rain is all that matters.

On the evening of the weeklong celebrations
of La Madonna della Luna primordial goddess
of the moon (and aren't we all
aren't Diana Mani Chandra You Me)

the spangle-bangled gypsy mother of god
magpie queen-of-queens in the rain-of-rains

is mounted on a wooden pallet shouldered
by muscled men in white jeans belted
with filmy red scarves paraded

onto a slick-deck boat promenaded
around the bay to the pummeling drums
and the rain rain rain. Rain

doesn't care about anything but raining
tonight in Porticello a cello-full
an earful an amphitheater of rain
a port over-full a carnival of rain

fragranced by the sea and everyone's tears
all the tears that might ever be shed.

On the other side of the storm-soaked sky
a whitening candle behind a parchment scrim
flairs a halo for the moon-bride who slides
along the oily tides pulling and polishing.

We raise our glass of moon-pale wine
in a toast to all things drenched—statues
boats and earth transformed and the sea
that doesn't even notice it's getting wet.

LIGHT FANTASTIC

La lumière est légère—light-bright and also light-
weight. Just entering into the morning light

and inhaling the sweet air is a light-
ning confirmation of the spirit. The light

divine made flesh, made arbor, made light-
blue sky, made fleur, made herb, soleil-light.

In these fields, farmers travail until twilight,
their old eyes wink, flicking star lights

while my dark American heart light-
ens, trips a beat and meets the fantastic light.

REENTRY

The quotidian's been made strange through absence
and this morning I'm opening the wrong cabinet doors.

I've returned from a dwelling carved higgledy-piggledy
into and out of a limestone hill, on and off since 900 A.D.,

while my condo dates from 1976 and suffers from the failure
of something called marblecrete. No opera birds

sing sophisticated melodies beyond no three-feet-deep
windowsills. But on the lake outside my sliding doors

delicious insects are luring the barn swallows so low
the jumping fish kiss them on the mouth.

I'm just sitting, calm, trying to *be here now,*
instead of caught transatlantic, when I notice

the lightening sky has revealed the contents
of my neighbors' balconies: plastic chairs

in a skin-crawling shade of caucasian flesh,
a row of metallic pinwheels blinding the rising sun,

rainbowed wind-socks, perhaps intended for the non-hearing
who might miss the incessant windchimes one balcony over,

a gas grill covered in what looks like a Darth Vader costume
and another who's come as Dracula, while the farthest balcony

sits dead empty in its foreclosure.
But somewhere over the lake, a seagull

flares its whiteness and puts on a demonstration
in how to cry, "I'm here! I'm here! I'm here!"

11TH AND PINE

This corner is no picnic,
no pocket park, no pea patch,
no Japanese garden of cherry trees
blinking blossoms onto the backs
of koi outfitted in gold lamé robes.

This corner's got *Queers in Space,*
Hoes on Rollerblades, Anal Cunts
with Strong Intentions sidetracked
straight up the wall of a warehouse
that ships and receives and provides
parking for its customers: bottle cap,
candy wrap, cigarette pack, molding snack—
parked not between the lines.

On this corner are bone-crossed bleeding needles,
infected palimpsested poster paper puke
from months and years of stapled *Cops in Capsules,*
stapled *Pussy Punks in Purple.*

A man in a night black coat lies flattened facedown
in the outerspace green of cornered astroturf.
He is sleeping. Or dead. He is tired.
Or drunk. He has had a heartache.
Or a heart attack. He's playing possum.
He just can't take it anymore.

On the other side of a grime-trashed loading ramp
an ungrown boy fetalizes
around his new suede sneakers,
a skinscraper sandpaper skateboard
pillow under his narcotized cherub cheek.

I am standing over this cherub boy,
above this black-night man, begging
to hold in both my hands a wand
of transmundation to transport them

into transparent beds in a house of hearts
where the man takes on the electric blue
of the last midnight sky,
where the boy's marigold hair
stocks his head with ponds of golden fish.

SIX

HIS MAJESTY UNDER A PARKING LOT

I think he wanted to be found, he was ready to be found,
and we found him. —Philippa Langley
on discovering the skeleton of Richard III

Skull off somewhere left of his neck,
                    it casts a glance
at the winding road of his vertebral cobbles
        as they detour around what would have been his liver.

Not bones of the Richard we love to hate
            but of the vulnerable weak and imperfect dead—
one glance at the photo and we want to weep.

            Canny and capable of ruling England,
                he wouldn't allow this S-curved spine
        arranged now on black velvet
                        to stop him.

Alongside the long-gash of an axe-headed halberd
                        to the crown of his head
        sits a U-shaped mandible.

Two leftover bone bits placed above it
            form a Happy Face,
                grinning not grimacing, directly at us.

He hid under sod,
            his feet missing altogether,
    under five centuries of other men's boot-soles,
                under a half century of parked Jaguars,
                        Aston Martins, and Bentleys.

DEATH IN BIG SUR

A log-jam dams-worth of disattached dead-matter.
Dead we are, they seem to be saying,
on the hillside, hilltop, bend in the creek,
bottom of the landslide, *dwell on us.*

Vines snake along branches, stake their livelihoods
so tenaciously that when they die they remain
right where they are, gyring the long branch,
their toes gripping years after death,
clinging as in life, and hell to remove.

The verdant, the golden, the mind-boggling beautiful
right alongside amputated limbs (arms to the elbow,
legs to the knee) leprosy'd or just deep-rutted,
washed down riverbed, culvert, gully and gulch.

In the Pacific Northwest, the dead are covered in moss
and the living too, should they stand still long enough.
In the Southeast, they're enshrouded in kudzu,
in the Northeast, silenced by ice and snow.

But here in Big Sur, the dead are exposed
by grays, by browns, by burl, by burn.

ISOLATION CONSOLATION

we're staggering now, just slightly
and we like it

caught out of time, out
of rhythm, way off rhyme

letting go of gravity, falling into
the dance, not a big solo,

no, it's a household's square-ish
round dance.

take hands, raise a glass, a bottle,
your arms,

thatch a canopy
for family to pass under.

as your feet grapevine, hands
grasp hands

in a finite circle of praise
praise

to the human this terrible animal.
in the morning

we'll feel low
beyond the adverbs quite very so

reel with me, every human
who's ever sought

through herb, blossom, bark,
to transcend, to end

up, not figuring out the compound
word of compassion

but merely to borrow
for a little while,

its heavy-soft wings
and embrace our fellow inmates.

WHEN THE GHOSTS LINK ARMS

after the Owara Kaze no Bon Festival, Toyama Prefecture, Japan

dance all night
counterclockwise
against the construct of time

tread thread weave the live
and the dead into a basket of birds

shriek of kestrels ka-raach
of herons careen flit blind as bats
turn on a dragonfly's dime

dance until the lightening
sky douses your fire
folds your knees
settles you down

the ancestors who borrow your body
return it at dawn
lying over you on the floor
like feather blankets

after three nights you wake
to find they are gone
you'll carry them weightless
for another year

on windy nights you will hear
their breath singing on the waves

they've got you on the left side
your heart or most of it

as they dance they fly

ELEGY FOR OLD FRIEND IAIN

Just as water arced between hose bib and grass blade
        at the moment car tires crunched the driveway gravel
and our neighbor's phone rang inside the summer window
        where a flapping gauze curtain almost caught a sparrow
who was in the midst of calling *Three Three Three Three*
        while a float plane scooped down to the lake
drowning out the hedge-clipper below and the siren beyond
        when inside the house the blades of the bedroom fan
began to turn slowly in reverse and I was humming
        How Are Things in Glocca Morra as I lifted
the clean white-load from the washer into the dryer
        exactly at that instant you left the body
and your throat rattled goodbye.

ZEN AND THE ART OF WALKING ON WATER

not the sound of a   lawn mower   weed whacker
jet ski   cigarette boat   dog bark
no neighbors conversing over a hedge
in decibels unknown to the human
voices of France or Spain
this summer morning in America
nothing but standers-on-boards
gliding over the lake slowly silently
and what looks like effortlessly
I see the paddle I do but
the flat boat and its upright figure
are a gondola and gondolier
a Kerala backwater pole boater
and no not Charon on the river Styx
not the old man searching for hard
pennies under soft cold tongues
no no you see of course not Charon
because no corpses no space
for the dead on a surfboard
and not night! sons of day not night!
golden sons and daughters gliding
smooth and forever over and under blue
their toes spread on almond-slivered white
these bronzed upright ones
have done it   done what Orion
and Jesus and Buddha are said to have
you know they must have read the book
practiced years breathing alert relaxed
striding out onto equipoise's single-point

CELESTIAL FANTASY FOR DR. ALZHEIMER

Will you vague angels
with your gauze wings angels
of not-knowing beauty

bear in innocence on a foggy night
the slowly fatal present
my dead mother and aunt

giftwrapped and placed
in your transparent arms
having tied to your halos

my not-so-permanent address?

After pressing your delivery
into my hands will you bourrée
the tips of your pointed feet

on the sprung floor of my brain?

If you spread your diaphanous gowns
and settle on my shoulders
will you whisper in my ears

the few things I need to remember?

COUNTRY SAUNA

Small talk drops away when we are beating
our backs ten to a room.

Sweat and live switches, their leaves still green,
and coals-made-incense.

Like a simple wooden chapel this Finnish sauna
where we women come in peace, naked,

offer a few words, leave grief in the anteroom
with our clothes, hanging on pegs.

Ancient women, only the stitching is new,
opposite me two breasts among three women.

A ruddy grandchild, dog hair stuck
to her wet skin, wanders in and out.

We go plunge in a lake.

FORAGING

I'm searching for something in the sea arrow grass
and maybe it's not the samphire, cilantro or goosefoot
I've been told grows here in the gravelly wind.

Something's craving sucked me from the fire-warmth
to smack me in the face with salted damp
and send my scraped hands and streaming nose
to search through peppergrass and stinging nettles,
among poisonous pokeweed blooming
near the lords-and-ladies who stuff
vermillion berries into their heavy hoods
while my toes turn the ivory color of corpses.

Partridge berry and blackberry brambles
entangle my slime-sogged ankles—they grip, I pitch
facefirst into the mud and before a sob flies up its wail
and curls into the mist like wild legume vines—
my nostrils gasp the perfume of ramps and rank garlic,
dandelion and borage blossoms, pungent watercress
and vanilla, the underscent of meadowsweet.

Today offers no particular reason for wailing
but the clouds are black on dark on pale,
sap sticks my fingers tight, dirt slap-paints my cheeks,
insects on leaves under leaves have adapted to my legs
and the smells—now wild fennel, now wood sorrel,
now goat's beard, spiderwort and deadly arum—
bind me fast with all foragers, plunderers,
gleaners and thieves, all of us singing out
our earth-engendered, earth-destined howls.

OFFERING

for David S. Buckel, environmentalist and LAMBDA lawyer who,
on April 14, 2018, self-immolated in Prospect Park, Brooklyn

Come liontail, swing yourself, arc, arch,
strike the match, its shocking bloom.
Flame-haired devouring eye, satisfied.
Lion-hungry belly, fill with him,
that you might spare the children.

You fire-breathing beasts of despair,
with all your heads and horns, your
long-tail scales fray the rope, tip
the hope-balance farther, a little
farther, toward *no more.*

Ting, the finger cymbal rings flawless
into the night. *Ting,* twice more.
Funeral flares fling embers into our ears
before the final silence, when children's
mouths will fill with ash.

Unbuckle him, unburn him, un-
fuel his futile flames, unfossil
the fumes, re-gold them. Fold
him in our unarmed arms.

MANIFESTO AFTER WENDELL BERRY

Expect the end of your nation as you know it. Plant alternate rows of weeping and laughter.

Loosen your mind. Drop it in the brown earth where it will take root or become compost.

Invest in the slow-moving, the tortoise. Plant white oak trees. Call the golden beetles eating the undersides of their leaves profit.

Praise horsetail, morning glory, dandelion. Have faith in weeds and all things uncontrollable.

Say your main crop is stars. Their constellations your formal garden. Ask who will harvest them.

Put your faith in ashes after wildfire. Prophesy flood. Listen to rain on the roof, on the broad and narrow leaves.

Say your main crop is talk. Count noise as profit. Donate your living ears. Plant giant voids. Gather the echoes.

Put your faith in rodents. Leave them the house in your will. Prophesy insects. Put your ears close to the crisp shells of cicadas.

Water your fields with tears. Call salt profit. Ask who will lick. Invest in dark colors. Harvest mushrooms, moss and mast.

Pledge allegiance to the most beautiful thing you can think of. Among so many candidates, how will you ever chose?

ACKNOWLEDGMENTS

Sincere thanks to the editors of the following publications in which these poems previously appeared:

Journals

The American Journal of Poetry: "Manifesto after Wendell Berry"
Avocet: "Zen and the Art of Walking on Water"
The Bear Deluxe: "11th and Pine"
The Briar Cliff Review: "Charming a Snake in the Woods"
Common Ground Review: "Celestial Fantasy for Dr. Alzheimer" and "The Loonies"
The Cordite Review: "The Flash" published as "Le Rayon Vert"
Crab Creek Review: "Barn Lit by a Duck Egg"
Dunes: "Great Blue"
The Ekphrastic Review: "1955 Rauschenberg Bed" (reprint)
Floating Bridge Pontoon: "Marquez Night" (reprint)
Flying South Contest Finalists: "The Ocean Is Raining in Porticello" and "Trilogy"
From the Depths: "Nostalgia for Dappled Shade"
Gold Man Review: "Elegy for Old Friend Iain"
The Halcyone: "When the Ghosts Link Arms" and "Floaters"
Leaping Clear: "Light Fantastic"
The Louisville Review: "Campana"
The Madison Review: "1955 Rauschenberg Bed"
Main Street Rag: "Come Live with Me"
Marathon Literary Review: "Empty Dress"
Midway Review: "Child on the Delta Shore" and "Elegy: A Dance"
New Orleans Review: "His Majesty under a Parking Lot"
North American Review: "Malheur"
North of Oxford: "Angel Hill Cemetery"
Painted Bride Quarterly: "Isolation Consolation"
Permafrost: "Hey Ho Nobody Home"
Poems2Go: "Marquez Night" (reprint)

Poet Lore: "Marquez Night"
Poetry East: "Hot Twelve O'Clock"
The RavensPerch: "Here between Day and Night"
RHINO: "Flying"
Roanoke Review: "Gloamish" and "Pearls before Swine"
SLAB: "Backbend"
Slapering Hol Press: "Sky Dance" and "Night Rites"
Sow's Ear Poetry Review: "Sleepwalker"
Stillwater Review: "Country Sauna"
Tampa Review: "The Tilemakers"
Tar River Poetry: "Frame the Moon"
Third Wednesday: "Equestrienne," "Foraging," and "Maryland
   Waterman"
Timberline Review: "Perfect Pitch"
The Voices Project: "Josephine of the Fields" published as
   "Grandmother of the Fields" and "Off Balance"
The William and Mary Review: "Infirmary"
WomenArts Quarterly: "Matisse Model"
Yemassee: "High Winds"

Anthologies

Dreamscapes: An Anthology: "Sleepwalker," Cherry House Press
Good Works Anthology: Aging: "Celestial Fantasy for
   Dr. Alzheimer"; *Good Works Anthology: Homelessness:* "11th and
   Pine"; *Good Works Anthology: Writings about Earth:* "Death in
   Big Sur," "Foraging," and "High Winds," Future Cycle Press
Forgotten Women: A Tribute in Poetry, edited by Ginny Lowe
   Connors: "Josephine of the Fields" published as "Grandmother
   of the Fields," Grayson Books
Mother Mary Comes to Me: A Pop Culture Poetry Anthology,
   edited by Collin Kelley and Karen Head: "From the Winged
   Virgin . . . ," Madville Publishing
The Poeming Pigeon: Poems about Birds, edited by Shawn
   Aveningo: "Hot Twelve O'Clock," The Poetry Box

The Poeming Pigeon: Poems from the Garden, edited by Shawn
   Aveningo: "Maple Seed Pod," The Poetry Box
Spheres and Canticles: "Broken" and "About a Delta," Propertius
   Press

Awards and Honors

"Appropriation" was the recipient of a 2018 *Florida Review* Editors'
   Award and was published in the journal.
"Child on the Delta Shore" was a finalist for the 2018 Patricia
   Dobler Poetry Award.
"Flying" was a finalist for the 2018 Joan Swift Memorial Prize
   from *Poetry Northwest*, and received an honorable mention
   from the Connecticut Poetry Society Contest.
"Offering" was the winner of the 2018 E.E. Cummings Prize,
   selected by Regie Gibson, sponsored by the New England
   Poetry Club.
"Night Rites" and "Sky Dance" were included in the chapbook
   Dubious Moon, winner of the 2017 Slapering Hol Press
   Chapbook Contest.

Deep Thanks

. . . to my beloved poetry sisters: Heidi Seaborn, Michele
   Bombardier, and Judith Skillman.
. . . to my mentors and colleagues: David Wagoner, Ken Wagner,
   Tree Swenson, Carolyne Wright, Jennifer Franklin, Margo
   Stever, Caroline Cumming, Christine Cote, and the poets of
   Volta.
. . . to Bill McNeill for his boundless support and love.
. . . to every one of my friends and family.

And special thanks to Seattle's Hugo House, my spiritual home
   and ad hoc graduate school.

ABOUT THE AUTHOR

credit: Ellen Skugstad

Lillo Way's chapbook, *Dubious Moon*, won the Hudson Valley Writers Center's Slapering Hol Chapbook Contest and was published in 2018. Her writing has appeared in *New Letters, Poet Lore, North American Review, New Orleans Review, Tampa Review, Louisville Review, Poetry East,* among others. Way has received grants from the National Endowment for the Arts, New York State Council on the Arts, and the Geraldine R. Dodge Foundation for her choreographic work involving poetry.

www.lilloway.com

SHANTI ARTS

NATURE · ART · SPIRIT

Please visit us online
to browse our entire book catalog,
including poetry collections and fiction,
books on travel, nature, healing, art,
photography, and more.

Also take a look at our highly
regarded art and literary journal,
Still Point Arts Quarterly, which
may be downloaded for free.

www.shantiarts.com

CPSIA information can be obtained
at www.ICGtesting.com
Printed in the USA
BVHW022305240621
609930BV00001B/2